KUMON®
MATH. READING. SUCCESS.

D0473270

What is Kumon?

Kumon is the world's largest supplemental education provider and a leader in producing outstanding results. After-school programs in math and reading at Kumon Centers around the globe have been helping children succeed for 50 years.

Kumon Workbooks represent just a fraction of our complete curriculum of preschool-to-college-level material assigned at Kumon Centers under the supervision of trained Kumon Instructors.

The Kumon Method enables each child to progress successfully by practicing material until concepts are mastered and advancing in small, manageable increments. Instructors carefully assign materials and pace advancement according to the strengths and needs of each individual student.

Students usually attend a Kumon Center twice a week and practice at home the other five days. Assignments take about twenty minutes.

Kumon helps students of all ages and abilities master the basics, improve concentration and study habits, and build confidence.

How did Kumon begin?

IT ALL BEGAN IN JAPAN 50 YEARS AGO when a parent and teacher named Toru Kumon found a way to help his son Takeshi do better in school. At the prompting of his wife, he created a series of short assignments that his son could complete successfully in less than 20 minutes a day and that would ultimately make high school math easy. Because each was just a bit more challenging than the last, Takeshi was able to master the skills and gain the confidence to keep advancing.

This unique self-learning method was so successful that Toru's son was able to do calculus by the time he was in the sixth grade. Understanding the value of good reading comprehension, Mr. Kumon then developed a reading program employing the same method. His programs are the basis and inspiration of those offered at Kumon Centers today under the expert guidance of professional Kumon Instructors.

Mr. Toru Kumon
Founder of Kumon

What can Kumon do for my child?

Kumon is geared to children of all ages and skill levels. Whether you want to give your child a leg up in his or her schooling, build a strong foundation for future studies or address a possible learning problem, Kumon provides an effective program for developing key learning skills given the strengths and needs of each individual child.

What makes Kumon so different?

Kumon uses neither a classroom model nor a tutoring approach. It's designed to facilitate self-acquisition of the skills and study habits needed to improve academic performance. This empowers children to succeed on their own, giving them a sense of accomplishment that fosters further achievement. Whether for remedial work or enrichment, a child advances according to individual ability and initiative to reach his or her full potential. Kumon is not only effective, but also surprisingly affordable.

What is the role of the Kumon Instructor?

Kumon Instructors regard themselves more as mentors or coaches than teachers in the traditional sense. Their principal role is to provide the direction, support and encouragement that will guide the student to performing at 100% of his or her potential. Along with their rigorous training in the Kumon Method, all Kumon Instructors share a passion for education and an earnest desire to help children succeed.

KUMON FOSTERS:

- A mastery of the basics of reading and math
- Improved concentration and study habits
- Increased self-discipline and self-confidence
- A proficiency in material at every level
- Performance to each student's full potential
- A sense of accomplishment

▶▶ GETTING STARTED IS EASY. Just call us at 877.586.6671 or visit kumon.com to request our free brochure and find a Kumon Center near you. We'll direct you to an Instructor who will be happy to speak with you about how Kumon can address your child's particular needs and arrange a free placement test. There are more than 1,700 Kumon Centers in the U.S. and Canada, and students may enroll at any time throughout the year, even summer. Contact us today.

FIND OUT MORE ABOUT KUMON MATH & READING CENTERS.
Receive a free copy of our parent guide, *Every Child an Achiever,* by visiting
kumon.com/go.survey or calling 877.586.6671

1 Writing Numbers

1 to 12

Name

Date

■ Trace the numbers in each ◯.

■ Trace the numbers in each ☐.

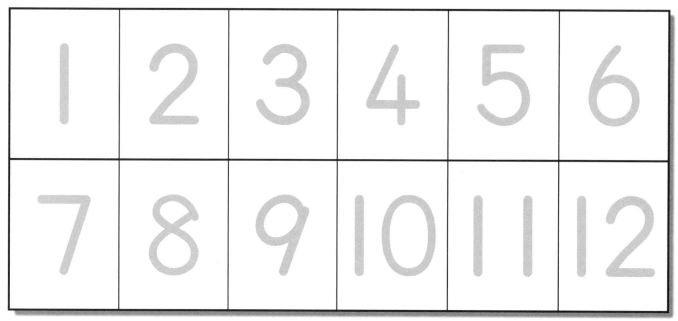

| 1 | 2 | 3 | 4 | 5 | 6 |
| 7 | 8 | 9 | 10 | 11 | 12 |

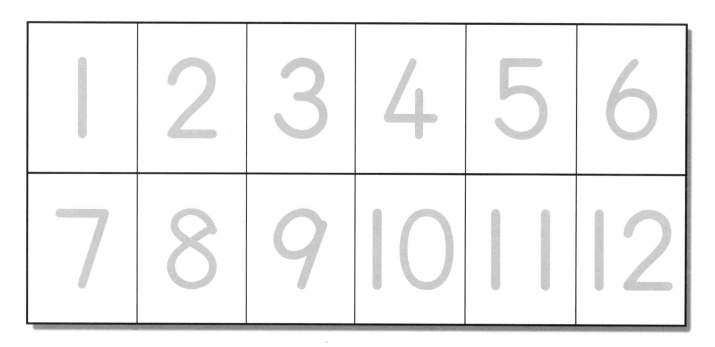

| 1 | 2 | 3 | 4 | 5 | 6 |
| 7 | 8 | 9 | 10 | 11 | 12 |

2 **Writing Numbers**
1 to 12

■ Fill in the missing numbers in each ◯.

■ Fill in the missing numbers in each ☐.

1	2	3		5	
7		9		11	

1	2		4		6
	8		10		12

3 Writing Numbers
1 to 12

Name

Date

■ Fill in the missing numbers in each ◯.

■ Fill in the missing numbers in each ☐.

1		3	4		
	8		10	11	

	2			5	6
7		9			12

Writing Numbers

1 to 12

■ Write the numbers from 1 to 12.

■ Write the numbers from 1 to 12.

	1	2	3	4	5	6
	7	8	9	10	11	12

	1	2	3		

5 What Time Is It?

1 o'clock to 2 o'clock

Name

Date

■ Look at the clock. Then trace the time in the ☐.

| o'clock

■Look at the clock. Then trace the time in the ☐ .

2 o'clock

What Time Is It?

3 o'clock to 6 o'clock

Name

Date

■ Look at each clock. Then trace the time in each ☐.

3 o'clock

4 o'clock

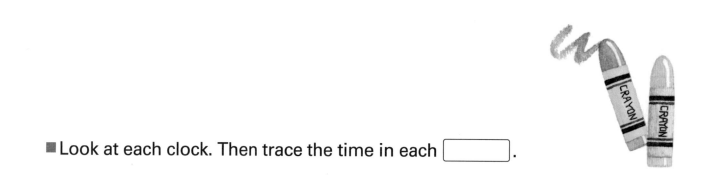

■Look at each clock. Then trace the time in each ▢.

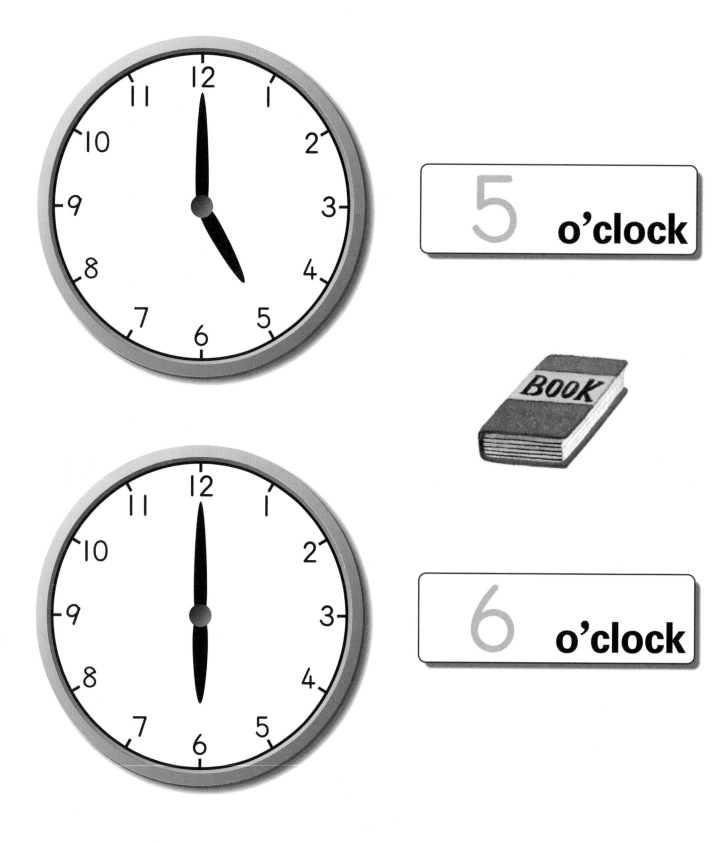

5 o'clock

6 o'clock

7 What Time Is It?

7 o'clock to 12 o'clock

■ Look at each clock. Then trace the time in each ⬚ .

7 o'clock

8 o'clock

9 o'clock

■Look at each clock. Then trace the time in each ☐.

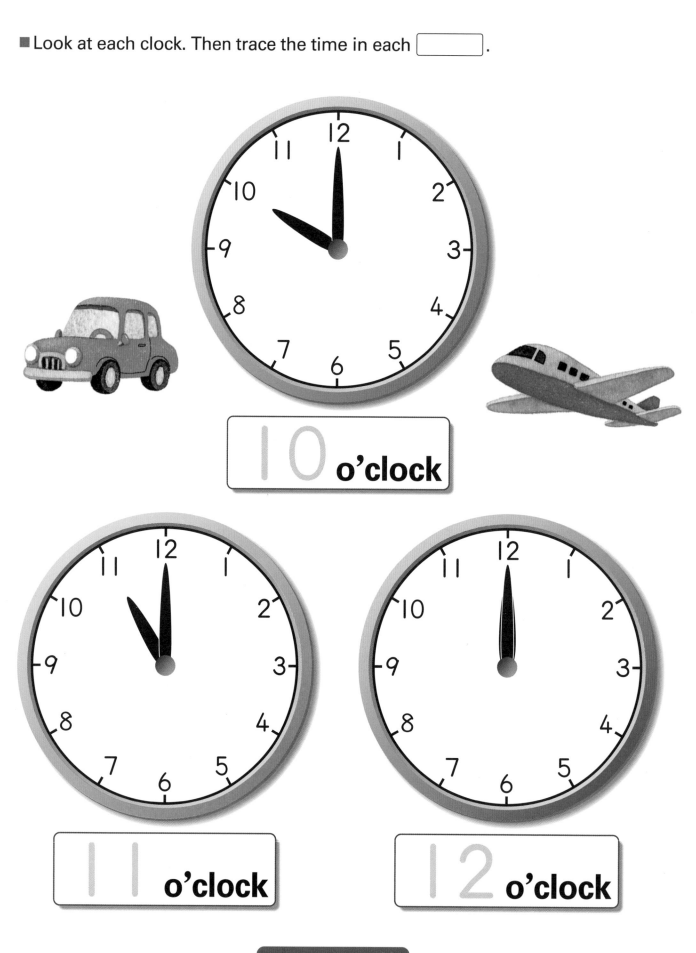

10 o'clock

11 o'clock

12 o'clock

What Time Is It?
1 o'clock to 4 o'clock

Name

Date

■ Look at each clock. Then trace the time in each ☐.

1 o'clock

2 o'clock

3 o'clock

4 o'clock

■ Look at each clock. Then write the time in each ☐ .

o'clock

o'clock

o'clock

o'clock

What Time Is It?

5 o'clock to 8 o'clock

Name

Date

■ Look at each clock. Then trace the time in each ☐.

5 o'clock

6 o'clock

7 o'clock

8 o'clock

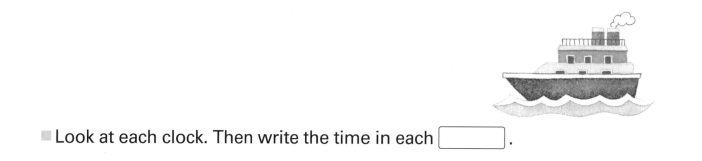

■Look at each clock. Then write the time in each ⬚ .

o'clock

o'clock

o'clock

o'clock

What Time Is It?

9 o'clock to 12 o'clock

Name

Date

■ Look at each clock. Then trace the time in each ☐ .

9 o'clock

10 o'clock

11 o'clock

12 o'clock

Look at each clock. Then write the time in each [ ].

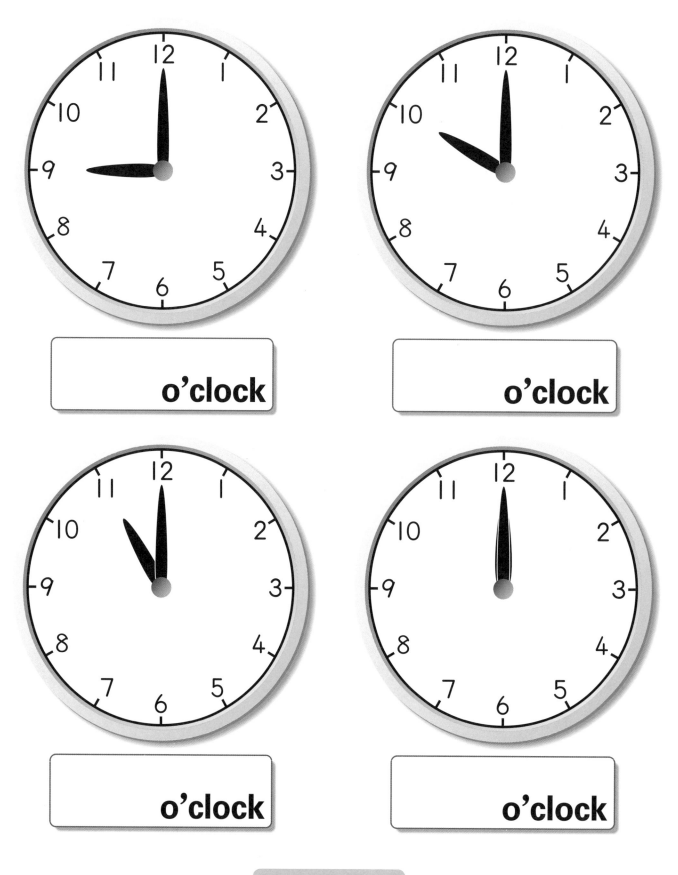

o'clock

o'clock

o'clock

o'clock

11 Review

1 o'clock to 12 o'clock

Name

Date

Look at each clock. Then write the time in each ☐ .

o'clock

o'clock

o'clock

o'clock

o'clock

o'clock

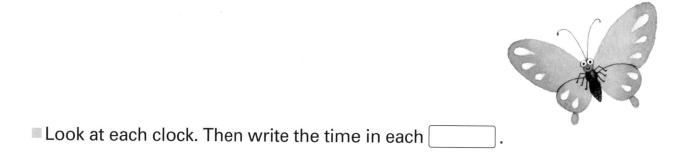

■Look at each clock. Then write the time in each ⬚ .

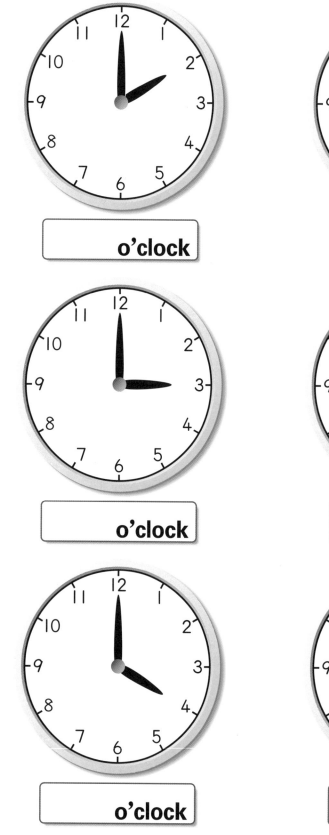

o'clock

o'clock

o'clock

o'clock

o'clock

o'clock

12 The River

Name

Date

■ Follow the river with your pencil. Stop and look at each clock.
Then write the time in each ☐.

o'clock

o'clock

o'clock

o'clock

Follow the river with your pencil. Stop and look at each clock.
Then write the time in each ☐.

o'clock

o'clock

o'clock

o'clock

13 The Long Hand

1 o'clock to 12 o'clock

To parents The long hand should point to the 12. The width of the line is not important.

Name

Date

■ Draw the long hand in the correct position on each clock.

1 o'clock

2 o'clock

3 o'clock

4 o'clock

5 o'clock

6 o'clock

Draw the long hand in the correct position on each clock.

7 o'clock

9 o'clock

11 o'clock

8 o'clock

10 o'clock

12 o'clock

The Short Hand

1 o'clock to 12 o'clock

To parents The short hand should point to the correct number for each question. The width of the line is not important.

Name

Date

■ Draw the short hand in the correct position on each clock.

Draw the short hand in the correct position on each clock.

7 o'clock

8 o'clock

9 o'clock

10 o'clock

11 o'clock

12 o'clock

The Short Hand

1 o'clock to 12 o'clock

Name

Date

■ Draw the short hand in the correct position on each clock.

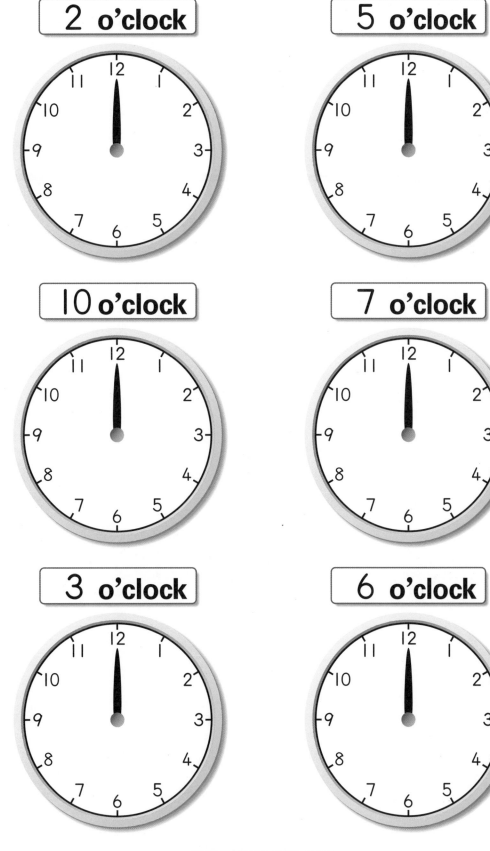

2 o'clock

5 o'clock

10 o'clock

7 o'clock

3 o'clock

6 o'clock

■ Draw the short hand in the correct position on each clock.

8 o'clock

1 o'clock

11 o'clock

9 o'clock

12 o'clock

4 o'clock

16 The Clock Hands

1 o'clock to 12 o'clock

■ Draw both the long hand and the short hand in the correct position on each clock.

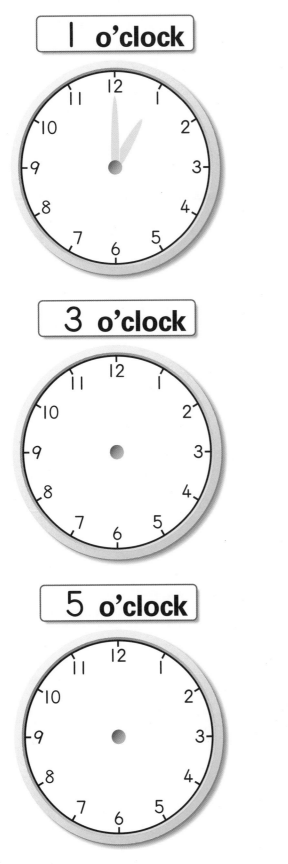

1 o'clock

2 o'clock

3 o'clock

4 o'clock

5 o'clock

6 o'clock

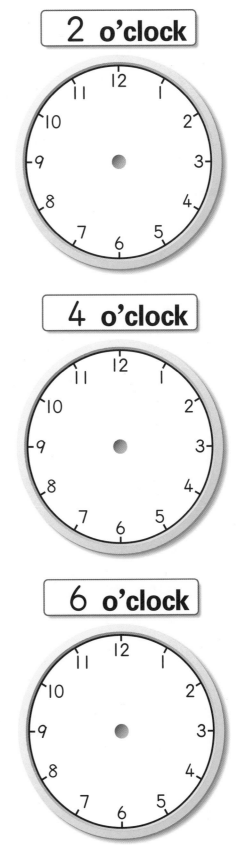

■Draw both hands in the correct position on each clock.

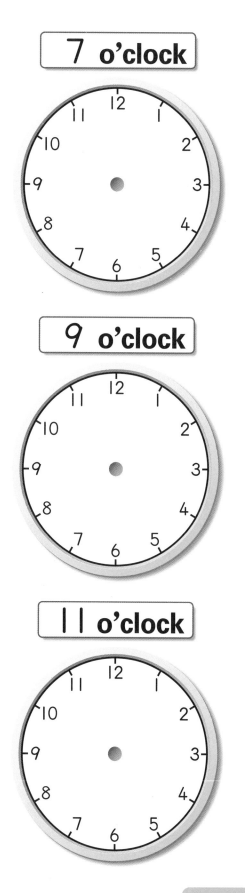

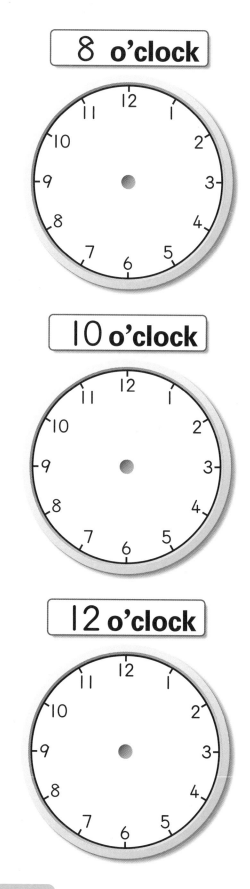

7 o'clock

8 o'clock

9 o'clock

10 o'clock

11 o'clock

12 o'clock

The Clock Hands

1 o'clock to 12 o'clock

Name

Date

■ Draw both hands in the correct position on each clock.

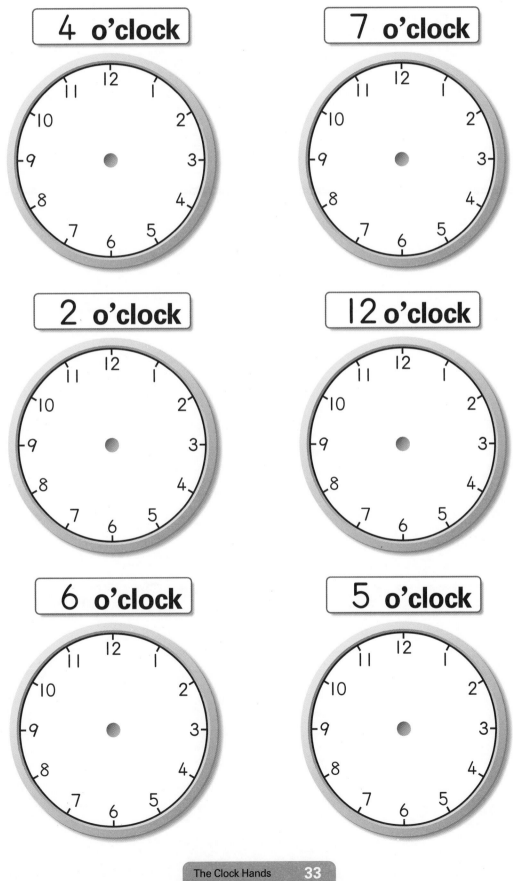

4 o'clock

7 o'clock

2 o'clock

12 o'clock

6 o'clock

5 o'clock

■ Draw both hands in the correct position on each clock.

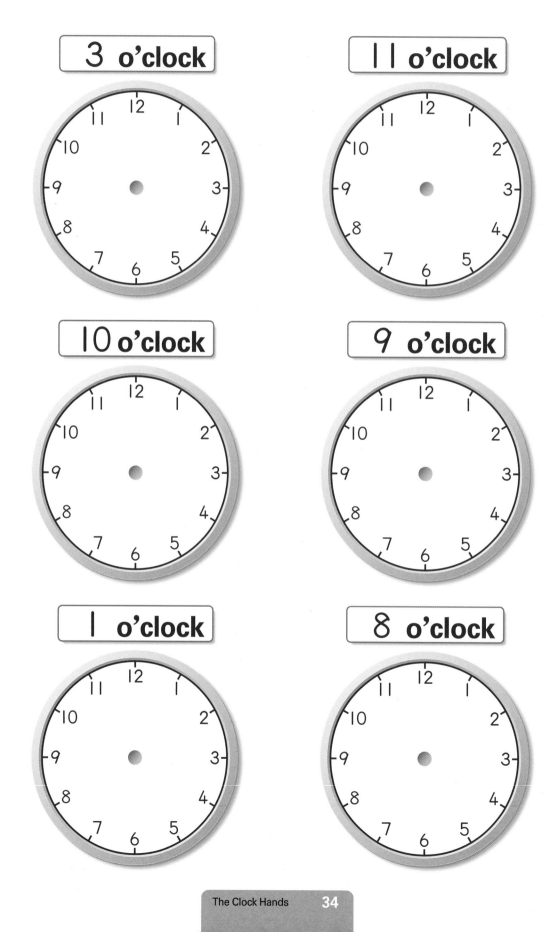

3 o'clock

11 o'clock

10 o'clock

9 o'clock

1 o'clock

8 o'clock

18 The Zoo

Name

Date

■ Follow the zoo path with your pencil. Stop and look at each clock.
Then write the time in each ☐.

o'clock

o'clock

o'clock

o'clock

o'clock

■Follow the zoo path with your pencil. Stop and look at each clock.
Then write the time in each ☐.

o'clock

o'clock

o'clock

o'clock

19 The Little Bear's Day

■ Draw both hands in the correct position on each clock after looking at the time below.

● The little bear wakes up at 6 o'clock.

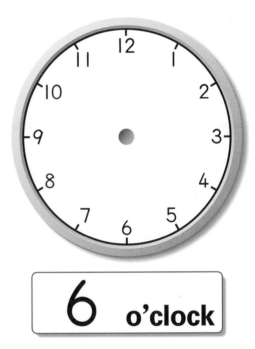

6 o'clock

● The little bear eats lunch at 12 o'clock.

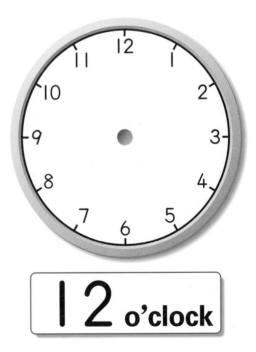

12 o'clock

■ Draw both hands in the correct position on each clock
after looking at the time below.

● The little bear takes a walk at 4 o'clock.

4 o'clock

● The little bear goes to bed at 7 o'clock.

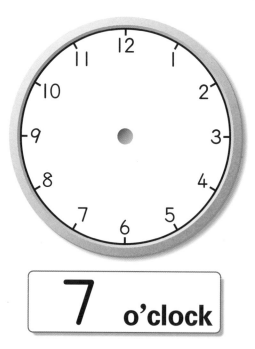

7 o'clock

What Time Is It?

Half past 1 to half past 2

To parents Explain to your child that halfway between 1 and 2 is called "half past 1."

■ Look at the clock. Then trace the time in the ☐ .

half past 1

■Look at the clock. Then trace the time in the ☐ .

half past 2

Name

Date

■ Look at each clock. Then trace the time in each ☐ .

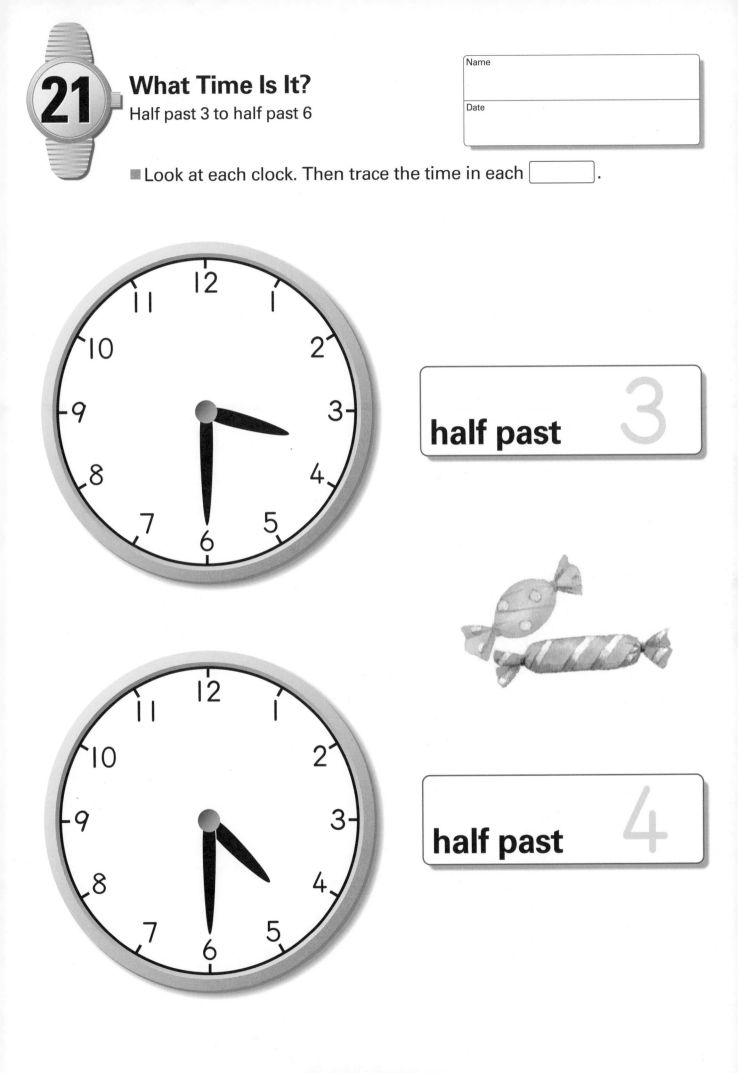

half past 3

half past 4

■ Look at each clock. Then trace the time in each ☐ .

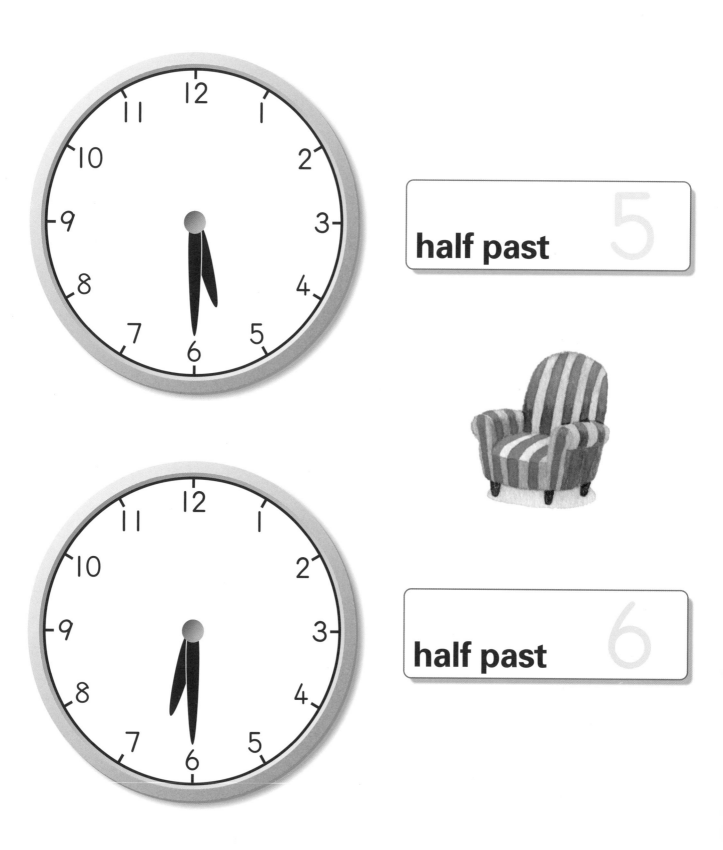

half past 5

half past 6

22 What Time Is It?

Half past 7 to half past 12

Name

Date

■ Look at each clock. Then trace the time in each ⬚.

half past 7

half past 8

half past 9

half past 10

half past 11

half past 12

What Time Is It?

Half past 1 to half past 4

Name

Date

■ Look at each clock. Then trace the time in each ☐.

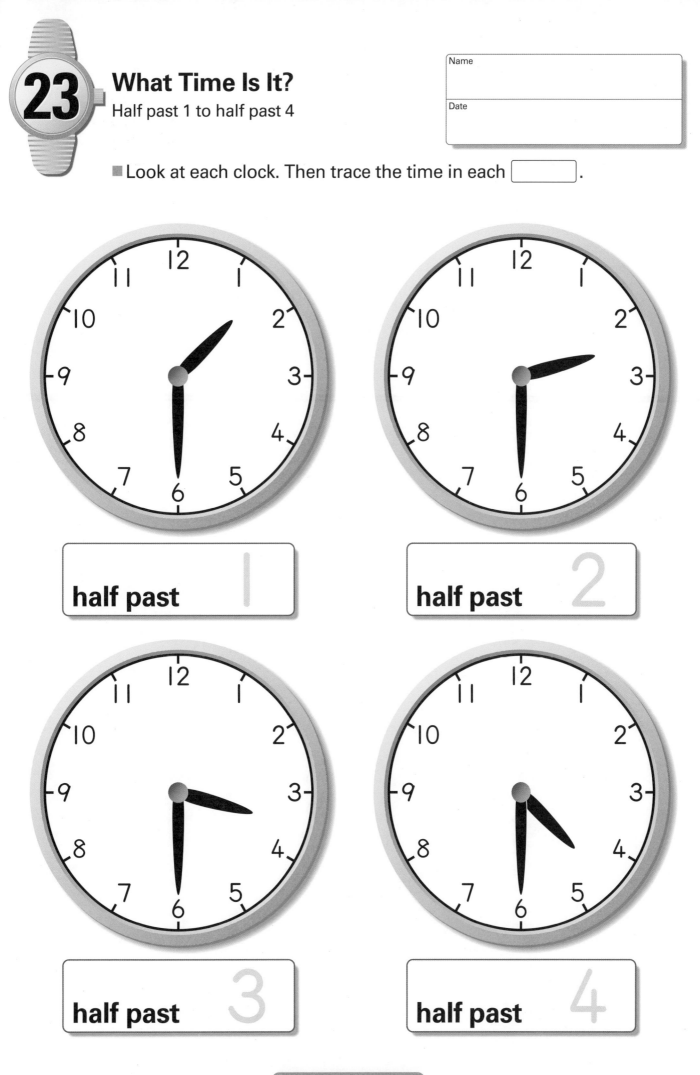

half past 1

half past 2

half past 3

half past 4

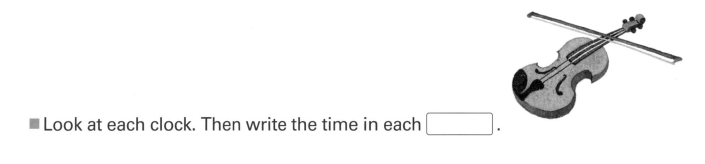

■ Look at each clock. Then write the time in each ☐ .

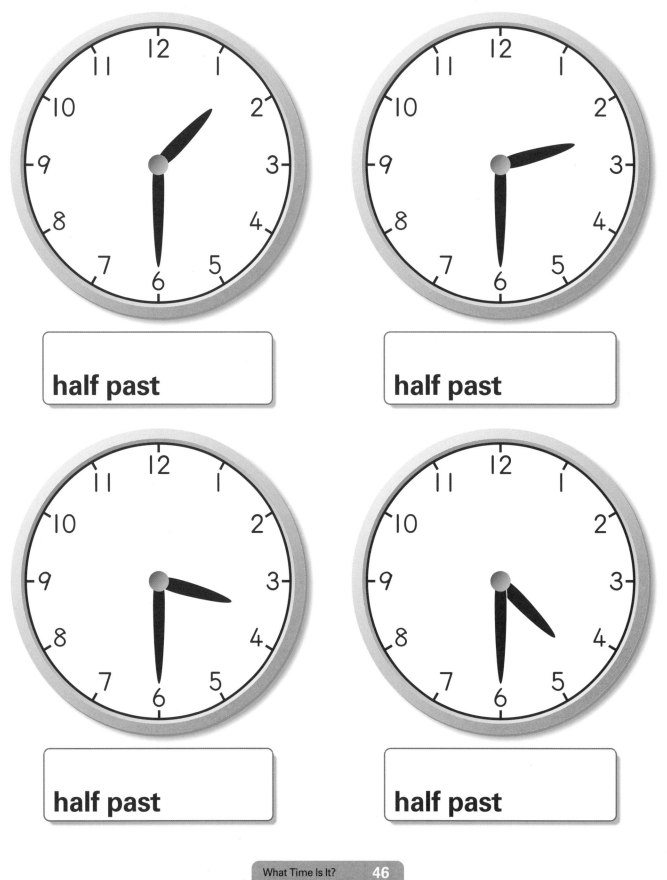

| half past | half past |

| half past | half past |

What Time Is It?

Half past 5 to half past 8

Name

Date

■ Look at each clock. Then trace the time in each ☐.

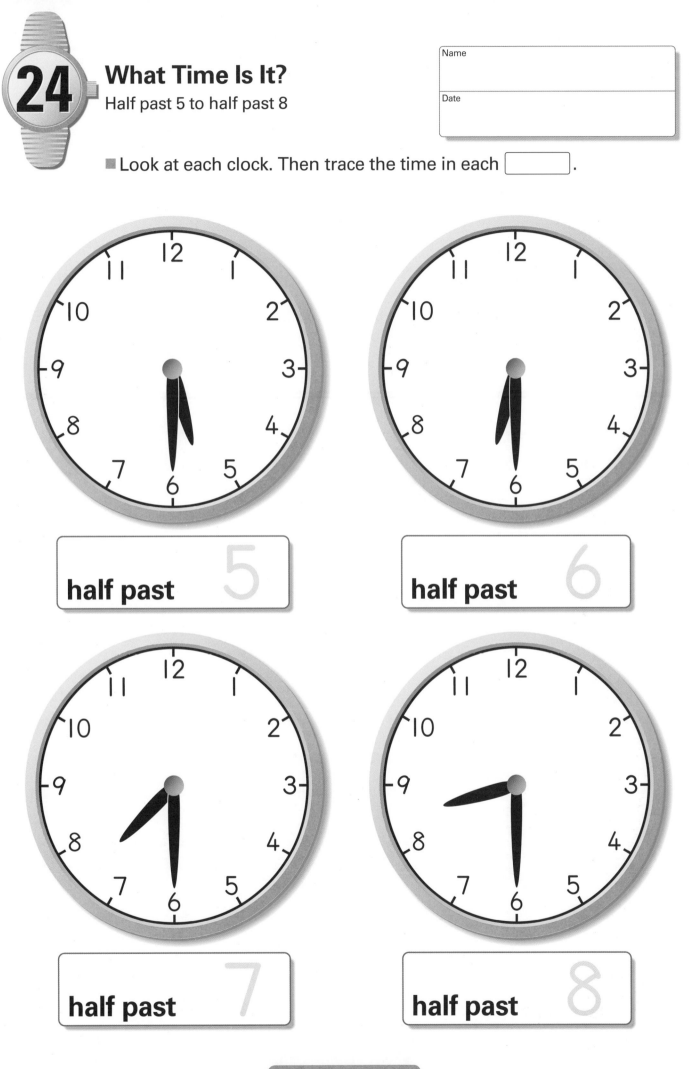

half past 5

half past 6

half past 7

half past 8

■ Look at each clock. Then write the time in each [   ] .

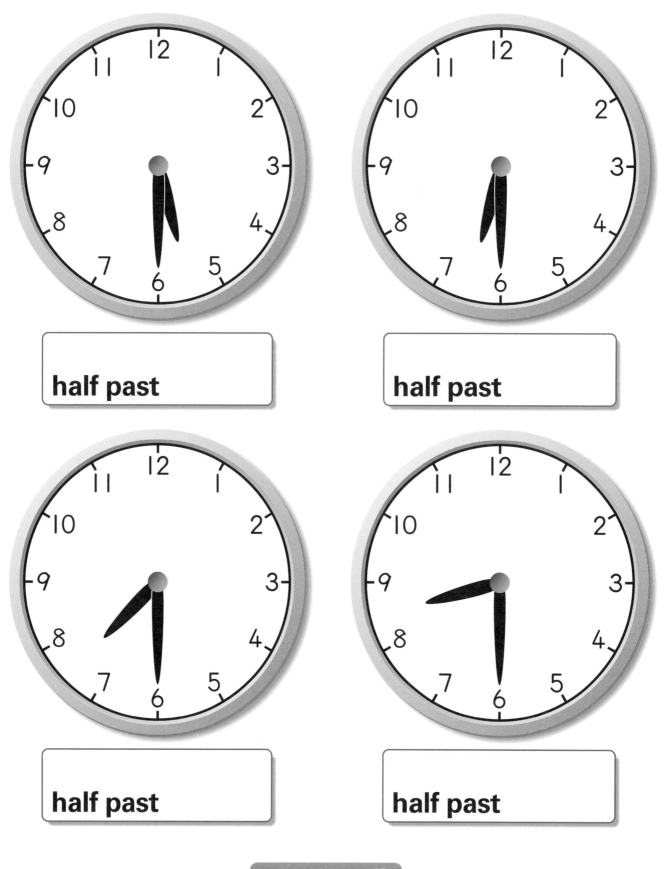

half past

half past

half past

half past

25 What Time Is It?

Half past 9 to half past 12

Name

Date

■ Look at each clock. Then trace the time in each ⬚.

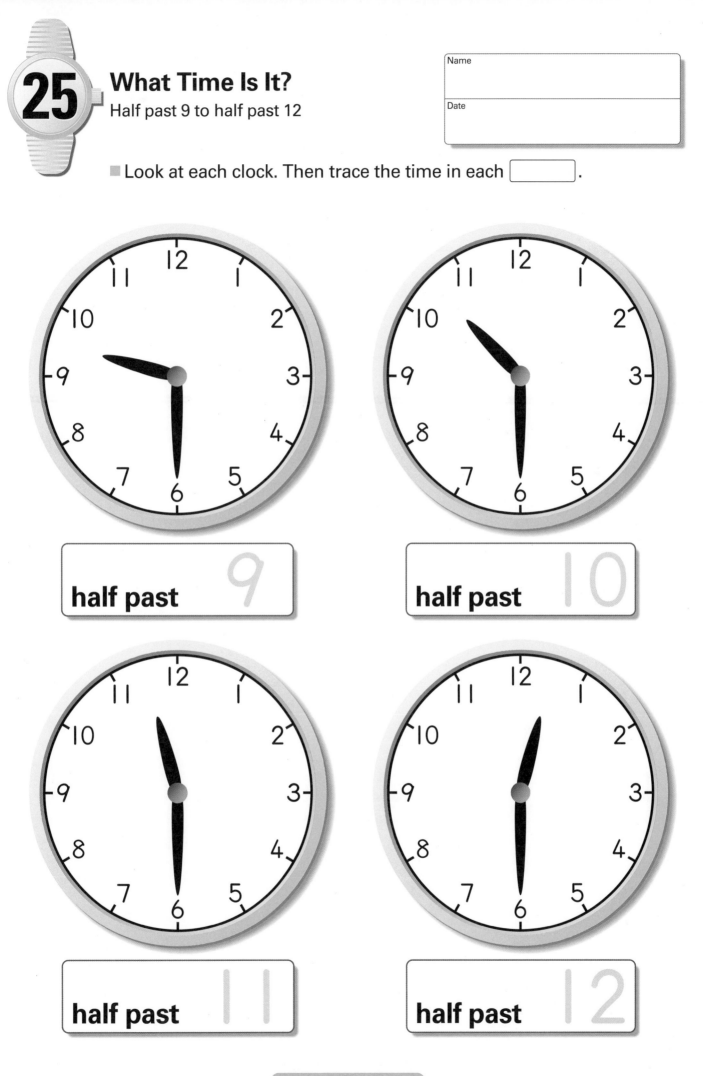

half past 9

half past 10

half past 11

half past 12

■ Look at each clock. Then write the time in each ⬚.

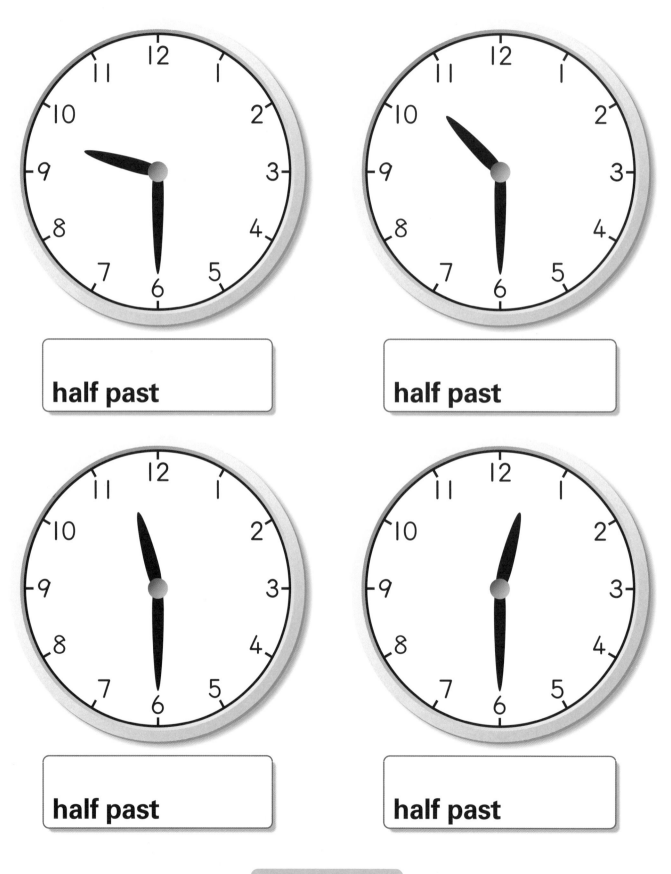

half past

half past

half past

half past

Name

Date

■ Look at each clock. Then write the time in each ☐.

half past

half past

half past

half past

half past

half past

Look at each clock. Then write the time in each ☐ .

half past

half past

half past

half past

half past

half past

27 **The Mountain Path**

Name

Date

■Follow the mountain path with your pencil. Stop and look at each
clock. Then write the time in each ☐.

half past

half past

half past

half past

■ Follow the mountain path with your pencil. Stop and look at each clock.
Then write the time in each ☐ .

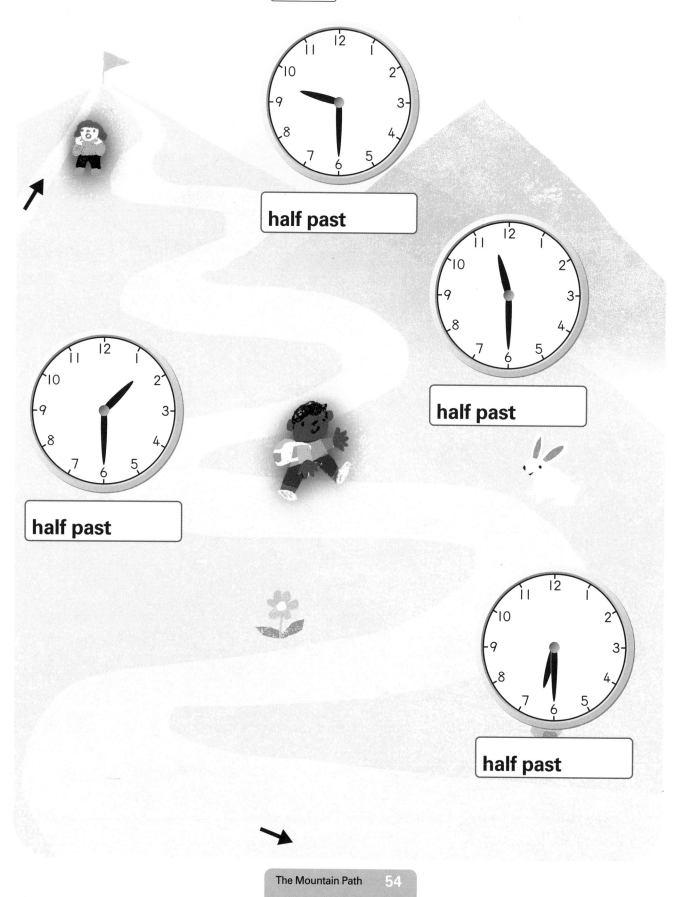

half past

half past

half past

half past

The Long Hand

Half past 1 to half past 12

To parents The long hand should point to the 6. The width of the line is not important.

Name

Date

■ Draw the long hand in the correct position on each clock.

half past 1

half past 2

half past 3

half past 4

half past 5

half past 6

■Draw the long hand in the correct position on each clock.

half past 7

half past 8

half past 9

half past 10

half past 11

half past 12

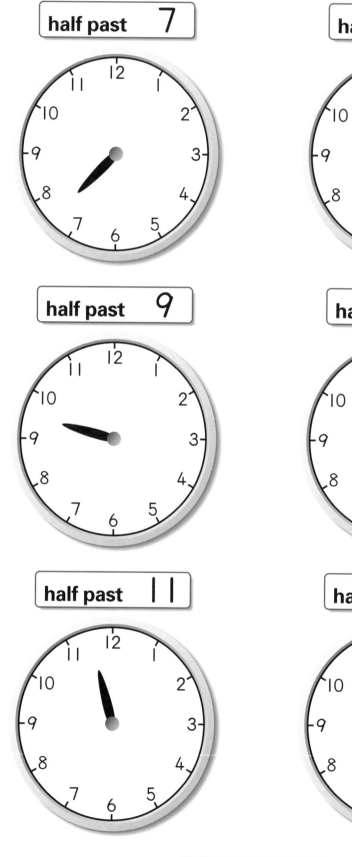

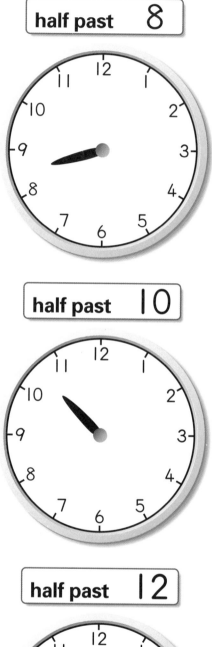

The Long Hand

Half past 1 to half past 12

Name

Date

■ Draw the long hand in the correct position on each clock.

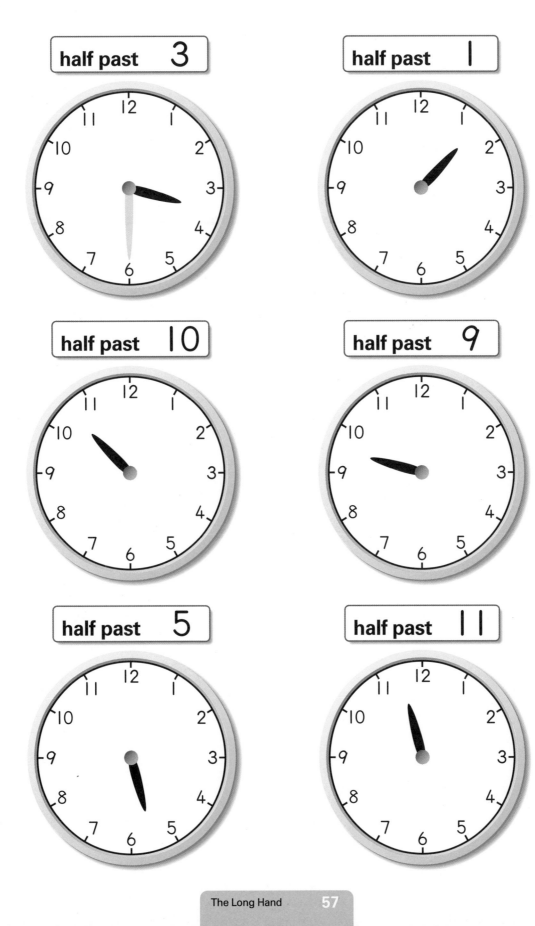

half past 3

half past 1

half past 10

half past 9

half past 5

half past 11

■Draw the long hand in the correct position on each clock.

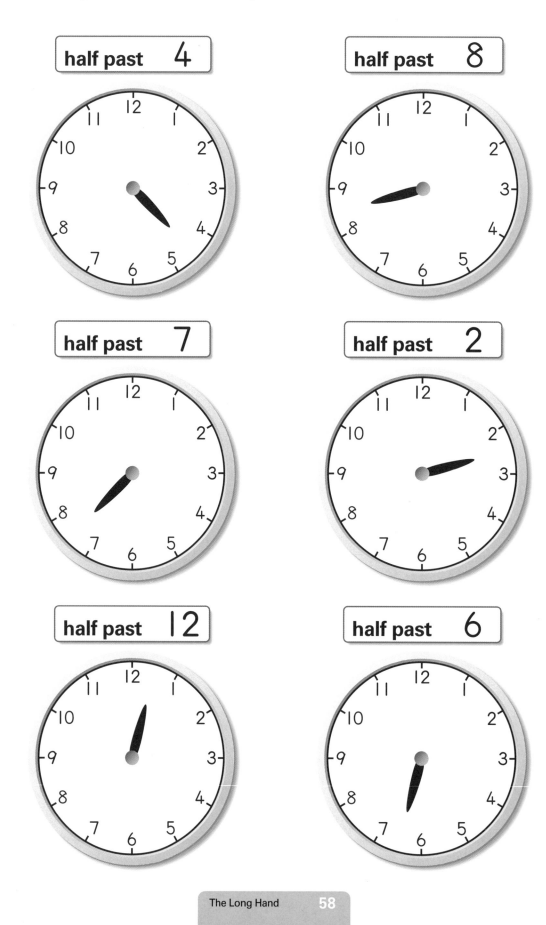

half past 4

half past 8

half past 7

half past 2

half past 12

half past 6

30 The Short Hand

Half past 1 to half past 12

To parents The short hand should point to the correct number for each question. The width of the line is not important.

Name

Date

■ Draw the short hand in the correct position on each clock.

half past 1

half past 2

half past 3

half past 4

half past 5

half past 6

■Draw the short hand in the correct position on each clock.

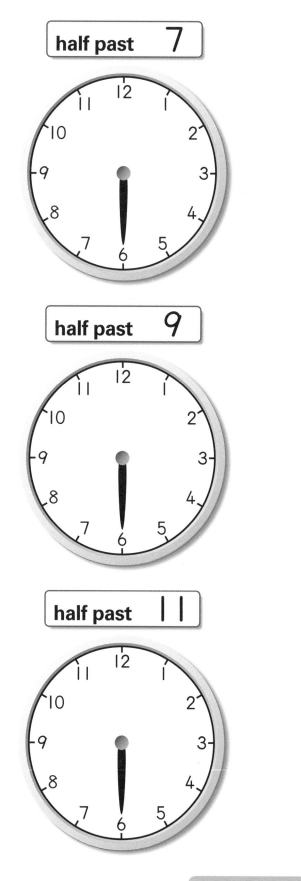

half past	7
half past	8
half past	9
half past	10
half past	11
half past	12

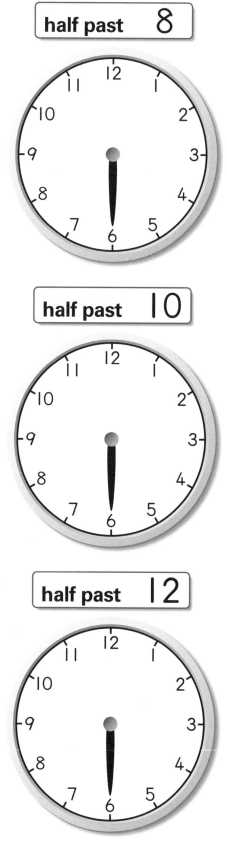

31 The Short Hand

Half past 1 to half past 12

■ Draw the short hand in the correct position on each clock.

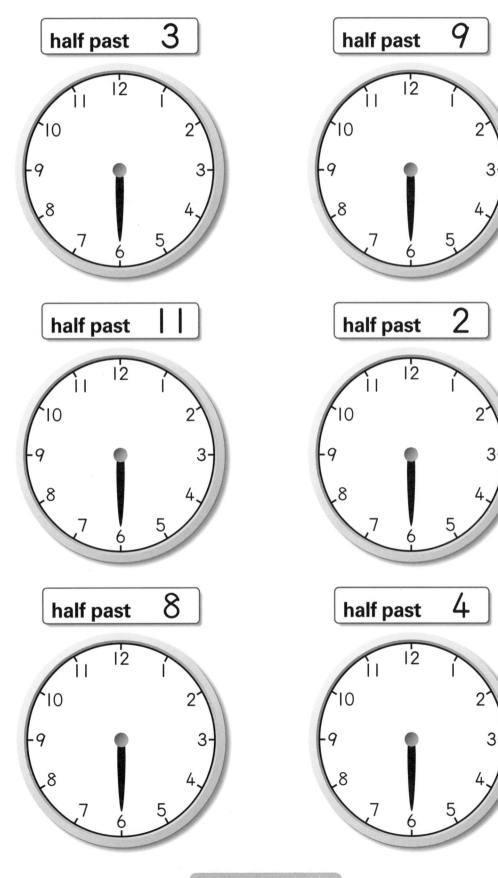

half past **3**

half past **9**

half past **11**

half past **2**

half past **8**

half past **4**

■ Draw the short hand in the correct position on each clock.

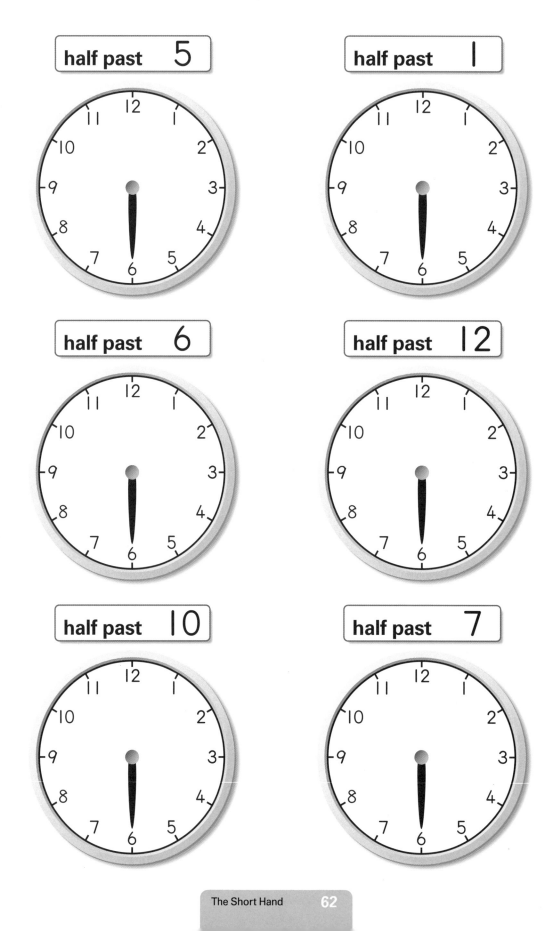

half past 5

half past 1

half past 6

half past 12

half past 10

half past 7

32 The Baker's Day

■ Look at each clock. Then write the time in each ⬜ .

● The baker starts to bake bread.

half past

● The bakery opens.

half past

■ Look at each clock. Then write the time in each ☐.

● The bakery is crowded.

half past

● The bakery is closed.

half past

33

What Time Is It?
1:00 to 12:00

Name

Date

■ Look at each clock. Then write the time in each ☐.

1:00 | o'clock

2:00 o'clock

3:00 o'clock

4:00 o'clock

5:00 o'clock

6:00 o'clock

■ Look at each clock. Then write the time in each ▢ .

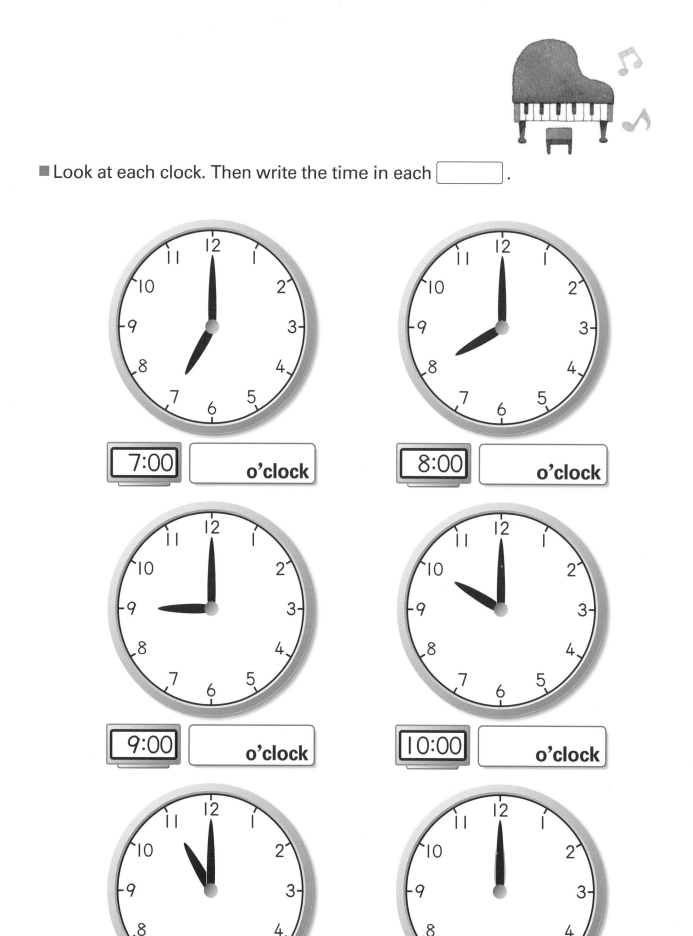

7:00 [   ] o'clock

8:00 [   ] o'clock

9:00 [   ] o'clock

10:00 [   ] o'clock

11:00 [   ] o'clock

12:00 [   ] o'clock

What Time Is It?

1:00 to 12:00

Name

Date

■ Look at each clock. Then trace the time in each ☐.

1:00

2:00

3:00

4:00

5:00

6:00

■ Look at each clock. Then trace the time in each ☐.

7:00

8:00

9:00

10:00

11:00

12:00

Review
1:00 to 12:00

Name

Date

■ Look at each clock. Then write the time in each ☐ .

2:00

:00

:00

:00

:00

:00

■ Look at each clock. Then write the time in each ☐ .

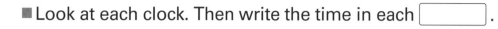

:00

:00

:00

:00

:00

:00

36

What Time Is It?

1:30 to 12:30

Name

Date

■ Look at each clock. Then write the time in each ☐.

1:30 | **half past** |

2:30 | **half past**

3:30 | **half past**

4:30 | **half past**

5:30 | **half past**

6:30 | **half past**

■Look at each clock. Then write the time in each ▢ .

7:30	half past
8:30	half past
9:30	half past
10:30	half past
11:30	half past
12:30	half past

What Time Is It?

1:30 to 12:30

Name

Date

■ Look at each clock. Then trace the time in each ☐.

1:30

2:30

3:30

4:30

5:30

6:30

■Look at each clock. Then trace the time in each ☐.

7:30

9:30

11:30

8:30

10:30

12:30

Name

Date

■ Look at each clock. Then write the time in each ☐ .

6 :30

:30

:30

:30

:30

:30

■ Look at each clock. Then write the time in each ☐ .

| :30 |

| :30 |

| :30 |

| :30 |

| :30 |

| :30 |

My Day

Write your name.

by

To parents   The phrase "o'clock" is printed in the answer boxes below. If your child would like to use "half past" to answer, please write that phrase in the box for him or her.

Write the time in each [ ] and then draw the hands on each clock.

■ What time do you wake up?

o'clock

■ What time do you eat breakfast?

o'clock

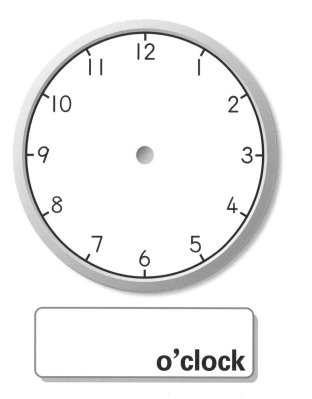

o'clock

■ What time do you go to school?

■ What time do you eat lunch?

o'clock

o'clock

What time do you leave school?

What time do you eat dinner?

o'clock

My Day

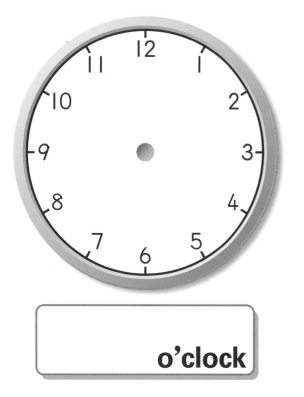

o'clock

■ What time do you take a bath?

■ What time do you go to bed?

o'clock

KUMON

Certificate of Achievement

is hereby congratulated on completing

My Book of Easy Telling Time

Presented on _____ , 20____

_____
Parent or Guardian